How to Write
Writing an Argument

by Nick Rebman

FOCUS READERS.
BEACON

www.focusreaders.com

Copyright © 2024 by Focus Readers®, Mendota Heights, MN 55120. All rights reserved. No part of this book may be reproduced or utilized in any form or by any means without written permission from the publisher.

Focus Readers is distributed by North Star Editions:
sales@northstareditions.com | 888-417-0195

Produced for Focus Readers by Red Line Editorial.

Photographs ©: Shutterstock Images, cover, 1, 8, 11, 13, 17, 19, 22, 27, 29; iStockphoto, 4, 7, 20–21; Red Line Editorial, 14, 24–25

Library of Congress Cataloging-in-Publication Data
Names: Rebman, Nick, author.
Title: Writing an argument / by Nick Rebman.
Description: Mendota Heights, MN : Focus Readers, 2024. | Series: How to write | Includes index. | Audience: Grades 2-3
Identifiers: LCCN 2023029417 (print) | LCCN 2023029418 (ebook) | ISBN 9798889980254 (hardcover) | ISBN 9798889980681 (paperback) | ISBN 9798889981510 (pdf) | ISBN 9798889981114 (ebook)
Subjects: LCSH: Persuasion (Rhetoric)--Juvenile literature. | Composition (Language arts)--Juvenile literature. | English language--Composition and exercises--Juvenile literature.
Classification: LCC P301.5.P47 R426 2024 (print) | LCC P301.5.P47 (ebook) | DDC 808--dc23/eng/20230728
LC record available at https://lccn.loc.gov/2023029417
LC ebook record available at https://lccn.loc.gov/2023029418

Printed in the United States of America
Mankato, MN
012024

About the Author

Nick Rebman is a writer and editor who lives in Minnesota.

Table of Contents

CHAPTER 1
Helping Pollinators 5

CHAPTER 2
Gathering Evidence 9

CHAPTER 3
First Draft 15

The Opinion Section 20

CHAPTER 4
Editing 23

Focus on Writing an Argument • 28
Glossary • 30
To Learn More • 31
Index • 32

Chapter 1

Helping Pollinators

A boy is reading about pollinators. These animals help plants grow. However, many pollinators are dying. They have nowhere to live. The boy gets an idea. He wants his school to build a pollinator garden.

 Learning new facts can change how people act in the world.

The boy starts writing an **essay**. He wants to **persuade** the principal of his school. The essay includes several facts from the book he read. It also includes his **opinions**. He explains why he thinks pollinator gardens are important.

Did You Know?

It's important to choose a topic you care about. That way, you'll be more likely to persuade your readers.

 Butterflies are one important type of pollinator.

The boy gives the essay to the principal. She agrees with his argument. Soon, the school builds a garden. The boy is happy. His essay helped make the school a better place.

Chapter 2

Gathering Evidence

An argument aims to persuade people. That's the goal of writing it. You help readers understand why your idea is best. You may also go over opposing ideas.

 Sometimes, people have many ideas and arguments at once. It can take time to find just one to write about.

You may explain what is wrong with them.

Writing an argument has several steps. First, decide what your argument is. What is the main point you're trying to make? For example, suppose you are writing about homework. Do you think homework is helpful? Or do you think it's harmful?

Next, you'll need to gather **evidence**. This information will help show that your argument is correct.

 The internet allows people to find huge amounts of information.

Your evidence should be based on facts. It should not be based on opinions. To find these facts, you may need to do **research**.

After that, make notes. Write down the evidence that supports your argument. Try to find at least three pieces of evidence.

Suppose your argument is that homework is harmful. Your evidence should not be "Homework is boring." That's an opinion.

The internet can help with research. But be sure to use trustworthy websites. A librarian can help you find them.

 Stress from homework can make students tired and have headaches.

Instead, use facts. One fact is that homework causes **stress**. Another fact is that homework makes many kids dislike school. A third is that not everyone has the tools they need to do homework.

Many people like to go on walks. They look at different things. Some people like to look at trees. But I like spotting birds the best. That's the most fun part about walks. There are many reasons why.

One reason why spotting birds on walks is the most fun is because birds can fly. Humans are stuck on the ground. It is amazing to see an animal soar through the with its own body. Not many other animals fly, at least on walks.

Another reason is that birds can be very colorful. Some birds are all black, and other birds are red or blue. Many birds have several different colors of feathers. It is fun to see colorful birds flying through the air on walks.

Finally, it is a fun challenge to spot birds. That's because birds can fly very fast. When I go on walks, it's easy to spot trees. But birds are small and quick. That makes it more fun when I am able to spot them.

Walks are a very fun part of my day. They are different parts of walks that people like more. Spottin birds on walks is my favorite part. Birds can fly. They are colorful. Plus, it's fun to work hard to spot a bir Those are the reasons why spotting birds is the m fun thing to do on walks.

Chapter 3

First Draft

After you gather evidence, it's time to write the first **draft**. Your essay should start with an introduction. This **paragraph** provides some basic facts. But most importantly, it states your main argument.

 The start of a new paragraph is often pushed to the right. This extra space is called an indent.

15

For example, you might first say homework is common. This shows what the essay is about. Then, state that homework is harmful. This is your main argument.

Next, write a paragraph for each piece of evidence. The first sentence should introduce the evidence. You might write, "Homework causes stress for students."

The rest of the paragraph should support that piece of evidence.

 Try writing your first draft in a notebook. You can make changes easily or start on a new page.

These sentences will explain why the first sentence is true. For instance, you might write, "Scientists did a large study. They studied stress from homework.

They found it caused many students to be unhealthy." At the end of the paragraph, you can also include opinions. For example, you might say, "This stress is not okay."

Your essay should end with a conclusion. This paragraph reminds readers of your main argument. It also **summarizes** your evidence.

Did You Know?

If you use a quote, be sure to tell readers where it came from.

 Arguments often call for change. The conclusion can state what that change should be.

You can also add an opinion. That way, it will be the last thing readers see. For instance, you could end with, "Homework must stop immediately."

WRITE LIKE A PRO

The Opinion Section

Many newspapers and news websites have opinion sections. In opinion sections, writers try to persuade others. They discuss a wide variety of topics. For instance, some people write about politics. Others write about health or education.

Reading is a great way to become a better writer. So, read an opinion article. Then, think about how the writer organized the article. Also, think about the words the writer used. Did the article persuade you? Why or why not? Ask yourself what you would have done differently.

There are many different news sources in the world.

Chapter 4

Editing

Your first draft won't be perfect. And that's okay. The next step is editing. This is the time to fix any mistakes. If possible, set your essay aside for a while. That way, you can look at it with fresh eyes.

 Sometimes, a good night's sleep can help you edit your draft.

Editing has several parts. First, read through your essay. Does each paragraph flow smoothly? If not, you may need to reorganize your sentences.

Second, be sure to use linking words. These words can help connect your ideas. Linking words include *because*, *therefore*, and *for example*. Also, use transition words when moving from one paragraph to the next. These words include *first*, *next*, and *finally*.

PARTS OF AN ARGUMENT

main argument

introduction

paragraph

evidence

linking word

opinion

conclusion

Why Homework Is Harmful

Homework is common. Many students have homework every day. Some people say it helps students learn. However, homework is harmful.

First, homework causes stress for students. Scientists did a large study. They studied stress from homework. They found it caused many students to be unhealthy. This stress is not okay.

The stress also makes many kids dislike school. Students do not like to feel stressed. Students only get homework at school. Therefore, their feelings about homework affect their feelings about school.

Third, not everyone has the tools they need to do homework. Students might need the internet. That way, they can do research. But some families don't have the internet. It's too costly. Those students can't do homework easily. That's unfair.

Not all students are able to do homework. It also makes some students not like school. Plus, homework can be stressful. That's why homework is harmful. It must stop immediately.

You can also use language that will persuade your readers. You may start a sentence with, "Experts have proven." Then, readers will be more likely to trust you. They'll know your opinion is backed up by evidence.

Finally, check your spelling. If you're writing on paper, you can use

Did You Know?

You want readers to think you're trustworthy. So, it's important that your essay doesn't have errors.

Some people circle their mistakes to help them edit.

a dictionary. It can help with words you're unsure of. Or, you might be writing on a computer. Then, the computer can check spelling.

Writing an argument is hard work. But it can change people's minds. And that can lead to changes in the world!

FOCUS ON
Writing an Argument

Write your answers on a separate piece of paper.

1. Write a paragraph that explains the main ideas of Chapter 3.

2. If you had to write an argument, what topic would you choose? Why?

3. What is an example of a linking word?
    - **A.** introduction
    - **B.** therefore
    - **C.** draft

4. Why is it helpful to end your essay with a conclusion?
    - **A.** Readers will be more likely to disagree with you.
    - **B.** Readers will be reminded of your main argument.
    - **C.** Readers will be unable to understand the evidence.

5. What does **reorganize** mean in this book?

First, read through your essay. Does each paragraph flow smoothly? If not, you may need to reorganize your sentences.

- **A.** to put in a different order
- **B.** to state an opinion
- **C.** to research a topic

6. What does *transition* mean in this book?

Linking words include because, therefore, *and* for example. *Also, use transition words when moving from one paragraph to the next.*

- **A.** editing a draft
- **B.** proving an argument
- **C.** connecting two things

Answer key on page 32.

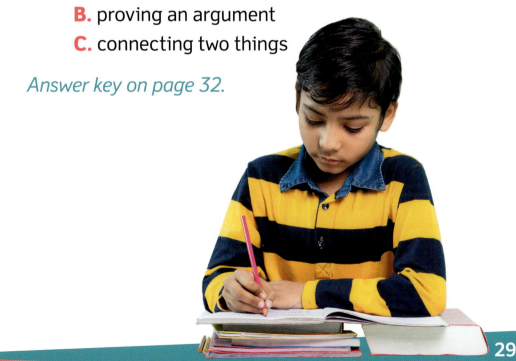

Glossary

draft

A version of a document that is likely to change.

essay

A short piece of writing that gives one person's argument.

evidence

Facts or pieces of information that prove something is true.

opinions

Ideas that are not based on facts.

paragraph

A part of a longer piece of writing that covers one idea and usually has more than one sentence.

persuade

To cause someone to think in a certain way.

research

The act of studying something to learn more about it.

stress

The body and mind's responses to difficult situations.

summarizes

Explains the main idea of a longer piece of writing.

To Learn More

BOOKS

Eason, Sarah, and Louise Spilsbury. *How Do I Write Well?* Shrewsbury, UK: Cheriton Children's Books, 2022.

Owens, Layla. *Is Virtual Learning Good for Students?* New York: KidHaven Publishing, 2022.

Rajczak Nelson, Kristen. *Letters*. Buffalo, NY: Gareth Stevens Publishing, 2024.

NOTE TO EDUCATORS

Visit **www.focusreaders.com** to find lesson plans, activities, links, and other resources related to this title.

Index

C
conclusion, 18, 25

E
editing, 23–24, 26–27
essay, 6–7, 15–16, 18, 23–24, 26
evidence, 10–12, 15–18, 25–26

F
facts, 6, 11, 13, 15
first draft, 15, 23

I
internet, 12
introduction, 15, 25

L
linking words, 24–25

M
main argument, 10, 15–16, 18, 25

N
newspapers, 20
news websites, 20

O
opinions, 6, 11–12, 18–19, 20, 25–26
opinion sections, 20

P
paragraphs, 15–16, 18, 24–25
persuade, 6, 9, 20, 26

Q
quote, 18

R
readers, 6, 9, 18–19, 26

Answer Key: 1. Answers will vary; 2. Answers will vary; 3. B; 4. B; 5. A; 6. C